The Rainbow

The Rainbow

Edel Kelly

Anne Dolan, Samantha Gustafson

Happy Ewe

For Mam & Dad.
Our world is a brighter place because of you both x x

For Síofra, Aisling & Shay.
May you never be too old to wonder at rainbows xxx

The Rainbow

Written by Edel Kelly and Anne Dolan
Illustrated by Samantha Gustafson

Copywright 2023 Edel Kelly

First Printing 2023

Published by Happy Ewe
www.happyewe.com.au

ISBN 978-0-6459032-0-1 (paperback)
ISBN 978-0-6459032-1-8 (hardback)
ISBN 978-0-6459032-2-5 (board book)

The Rainbow

I look out the window
and what do I see?

|4|

Beautiful colours
looking at me!

Across the sky

the arc appears...

... to let us know sunshine is near.

Colours of red, orange,
yellow, green...

... blue, indigo and violet
can be seen.

I look and wish
that it would stay

but alas it
goes away.

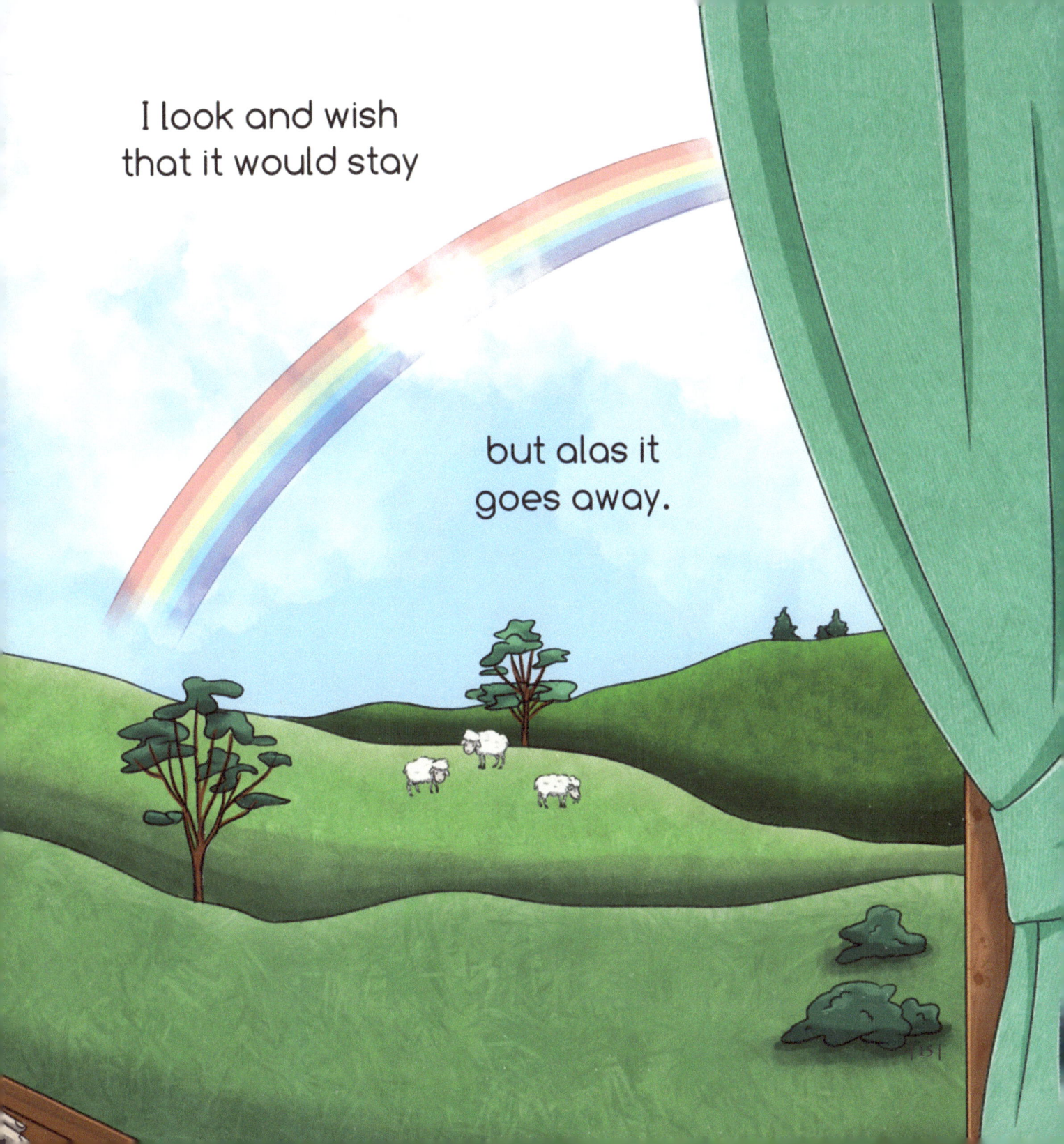

I've loved your
magical colour show.

| 16 |

Goodbye for now
beautiful rainbow!

www.ingramcontent.com/pod-product-compliance
Lightning Source LLC
Chambersburg PA
CBHW042027090426
42811CB00016B/1772